TopReaders

Dinosaurs

Robert Coupe

Contents

Dinosaurs lived on Earth long
before there were any people.
Many were huge. Others were
very small animals. Some
dinosaurs hunted their food,
and some ate nothing but plants.

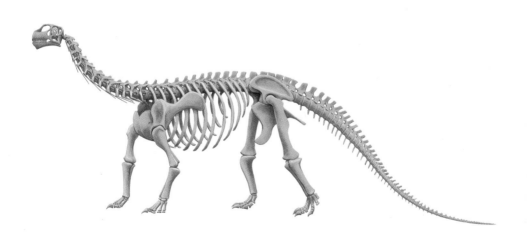

All Kinds

Dinosaurs existed for 160 million years.
They died out 65 million years ago.
We now know a lot about their lives.
In many places, people have found bones
and other parts of dinosaur bodies.

Tyrannosaurus

Triceratops

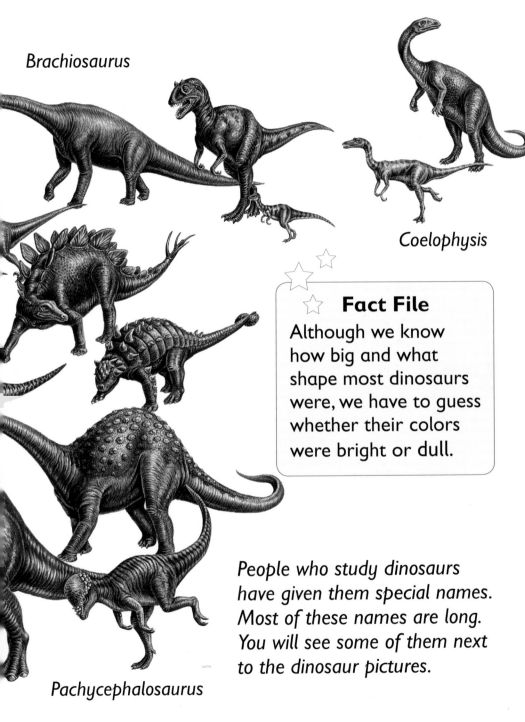

Brachiosaurus

Coelophysis

Pachycephalosaurus

★ **Fact File**
Although we know how big and what shape most dinosaurs were, we have to guess whether their colors were bright or dull.

People who study dinosaurs have given them special names. Most of these names are long. You will see some of them next to the dinosaur pictures.

Dino Babies

Just like birds, dinosaurs made nests
and laid eggs. Baby dinosaurs hatched
from these eggs. Many dinosaurs
cared for their babies in the nests.
They fed them until they could walk.

babies

*This mother Oviraptor is feeding her babies
another kind of baby dinosaur that she has caught.*

mother

Claws and Teeth

Many dinosaurs were fierce hunters.
Some caught and ate other dinosaurs.
Others ate different kinds of animals.
Most hunters had powerful teeth or claws,
and many could move very quickly.

Fact File

Some dinosaur experts think
Deinonychus had feathers.
The feathers were to keep it
warm. It could not fly.

Deinonychus lived and hunted in North America. Its long, hooked claws were very sharp. They could hold and tear apart animals that this dinosaur caught.

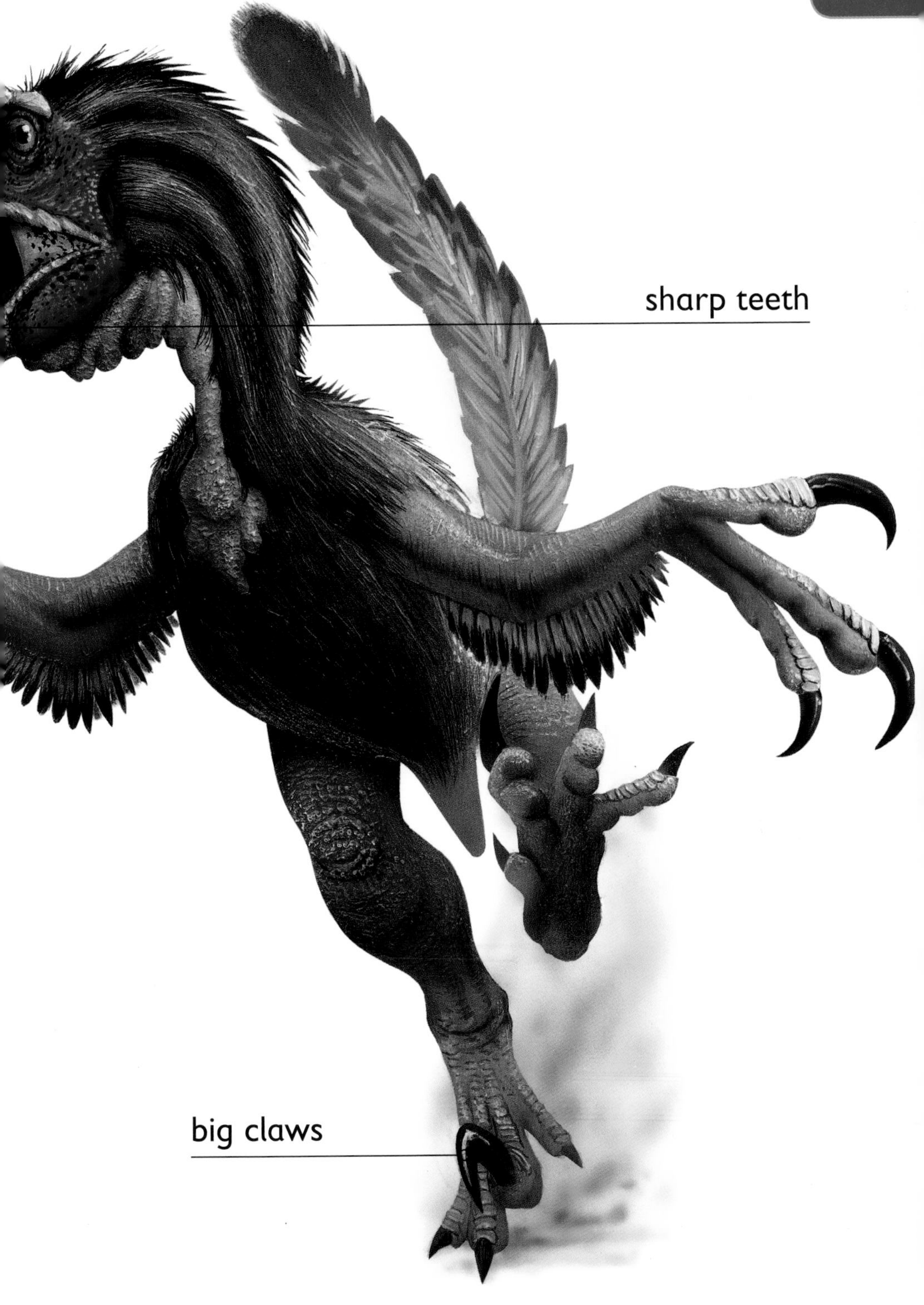
sharp teeth
big claws

Giant Plant-eater

While many dinosaurs ate other animals, most of them fed mainly on plants. *Stegosaurus* was a giant plant-eater. It had no front teeth. It had a beak that it used to chop off clumps of ferns.

sharp spike

Stegosaurus had bony plates on its neck, back, and tail. These helped to keep it warm or cool. It could use the spikes on its tail to defend itself.

bony plate

Three Horns

Triceratops was a very large dinosaur that looked like a modern rhinoceros. It had three horns on its head. It did not hunt other animals. It used its strong beak to break off the plants that it ate.

The three horns and the frill *of small bones on its neck helped Triceratops to* defend *itself against dinosaurs and other animals that attacked it.*

bony frill

horn

Mighty Meat-eater

Tyrannosaurus was large and fierce.
This dinosaur had strong back legs,
but small arms. It had four claws
on each back leg and two on each arm.
It lived and hunted in North America.

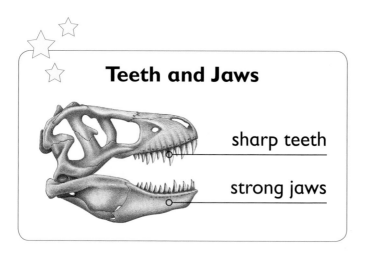

Teeth and Jaws

sharp teeth

strong jaws

The mouth of Tyrannosaurus was huge and it had long, sharp teeth. With its powerful jaws, it could crunch up the bones of animals that it caught.

big teeth

Neck and Tail

Diplodocus's tiny head could reach high into trees. Here its stubby teeth stripped off leaves. Most of the time, it held its neck and tail straight out. It was one of the longest of all dinosaurs.

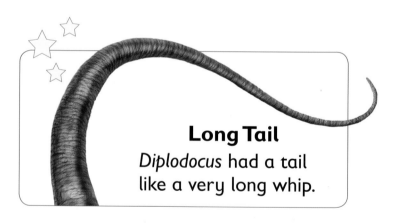

Long Tail
Diplodocus had a tail like a very long whip.

Diplodocus *had two long, sharp claws. It used them and its long tail to fight against dinosaurs that attacked it. Diplodocus ate only plants.*

long neck

Duckbill

The crest on *Parasaurolophus's* head was
hollow. Air moved through the crest
when the dinosaur called out.
This dinosaur lived in herds.
This helped protect
it from attackers.

duck-billed mouth

Parasaurolophus *belonged to a group of animals
that we call duck-billed dinosaurs. This is because
their mouths looked a bit like the bills of ducks.*

air moving
through crest

Fact File

This dinosaur's mouth
was packed with hundreds
of small teeth. It used
them to chew up stems
of the plants that it ate.

First Bird

Many experts believe *Archaeopteryx* was the first bird. It had feathers and wings. Its head was like the head of today's birds. It could probably fly, but stayed mainly on the ground.

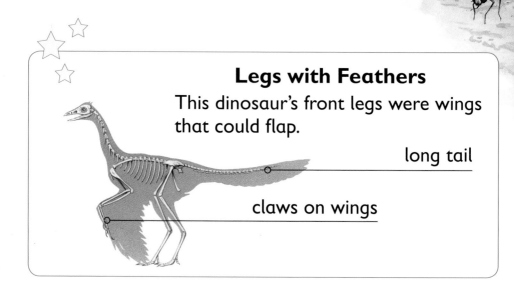

Legs with Feathers

This dinosaur's front legs were wings that could flap.

long tail

claws on wings

Archaeopteryx could run fast on its long, thin, hind legs. This dinosaur lived near a shallow sea. Insects and fish were probably its main kinds of food.

Fast and Slow

Albertosaurus was a big, strong hunter.
Gallimimus was a very fast runner.
On its long hind legs it could run away
from its large enemy. With its long neck,
it looked a bit like a modern ostrich.

Fact File
Gallimimus had eyes on the sides
of its head. Like most hunters,
Albertosaurus had eyes that both
looked toward the front.

Albertosaurus *had strong jaws and lots of sharp teeth.*
Gallimimus's *head was small and it had no teeth.*
It probably ate insects, lizards, and small mammals.

Gallimimus

Albertosaurus

Dino Bones

Most dinosaurs were large animals.
We know this from the skeletons
and bones that people have found.
Some, like this one, moved on four legs.
Others walked and ran on only two legs.

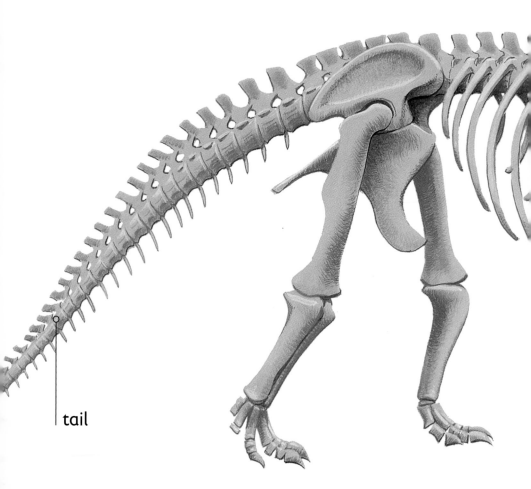

tail

This is a skeleton of Camarasaurus. This dinosaur had legs like huge pillars. These helped to support the great weight of the animal's body.

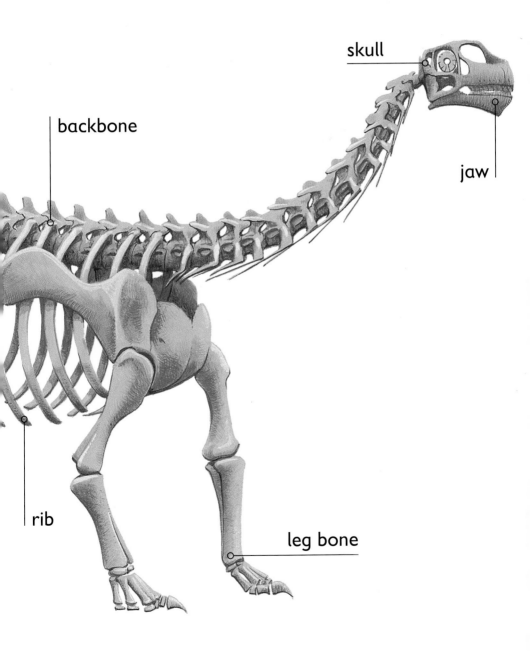

skull

backbone

jaw

rib

leg bone

The Dinosaurs Disappear

Sixty-five million years ago, a meteorite, a huge object from space, hit Earth. Dust flew into the air. It blocked out the Sun. This caused the dinosaurs, and many other animals, to die out.

Most experts agree
that a meteorite caused
the death of the dinosaurs.
A few believe that Earth's
climate became much
hotter, and this is why
they died.

Digging up Fossils

Bones and other parts of dinosaurs
are called fossils . To find fossils,
people dig in the earth or into rocks.
Sometimes they find a large skeleton.
Often, they find only small bones.

These people have found the bones
of two dinosaurs in a desert area.
They are digging them carefully
out of the ground.

Digging Tools

brush   trowel

Quiz

Can you unscramble the words and match them with the right pictures?

LOOPARPSAURHAUS   STANSONRARUYU

KELTSONE   VIROPRATO

Glossary

beak: a hard, pointed part of the mouths of some dinosaurs

climate: the kind of weather that a place usually has

crest: a part that stands up high above the heads of some dinosaurs

defend: what an animal does to keep safe when it is attacked

fossils: footprints, or parts of a dead animal or plant that have been in the ground for a very long time

frill: a part of an animal's body that stands out like a fan. Frills are usually behind the head.

herds: groups of animals that live or move around together

mammals: animals that drink milk from their mother's body when they are babies

meteorite: a very large piece of rock or metal that comes from space and hits Earth

ostrich: a large bird with long legs and a long neck, which runs fast and cannot fly

plates: pieces of bone or other hard material on the outside of an animal's body

skeletons: all the bones in animals' bodies

Index